the little book of

MOTHER'S LOVE

the little book of MOTHER'S LOVE

Raymond Glynne

ARCTURUS

PICTURE ACKNOWLEDGEMENTS

Ardea: 47, 50, 87, 93, 94.

Corbis: 23, 42, 58, 69, 71, 74, 78, 81, 85, 95, 96.

FLPA: 8, 13, 17, 20, 26, 48, 55, 91.

Creative Image Library: 86.

Getty: 32, 75, 77.

Nature Picture Library: 39, 40, 49, 52, 57, 63, 64, 65, 70, 76, 82.

Photoshot: 51, 60, 68, 89, 90.

Press Association: 10, 19, 22, 28, 31, 73, 79, 80, 88, 92.

RSPB: 66.

Science Photo Library: 59.

Shutterstock: 6, 7, 9, 11, 12, 14, 15, 16, 18, 21, 24, 25, 27, 29, 30, 33, 34, 35, 36, 37, 38, 43, 44, 45, 46, 53, 54, 56, 61, 62, 67, 72.

Superstock: 41, 83, 84.

ARCTURUS

This edition published in 2011 by Arcturus Publishing Limited
26/27 Bickels Yard, 151–153 Bermondsey Street,
London SE1 3HA

ISBN: 978-1-84837-761-5
AD001715EN

Printed in China

There are many powerful forces in nature, but few more powerful than a mother's love. It's a formidable thing, both tender and fierce, and it never falters or fades. As children we often take it for granted. Only as we grow older do we appreciate its capacity for protecting, nurturing, teaching and making us feel secure.

Mother's love is not planned or rehearsed. It is an instinctive response, unquestioning, uncompromising and unending. Well beyond childhood we continue to feel it, and yearn for it. And when it's there, the whole world seems a better place.

A mother's love is pure affection…

Sheer tenderness…

Total adoration...

What mother can resist her child's affection?...

And what child can resist its mother's?...

Love is making sure your children don't go hungry...

No matter how many mouths there are to feed...

And that they have plenty to drink, too…

Family mealtimes are a bonding experience...

A special moment between loved ones...

LISTEN AND LEARN

Children learn vital lessons from Mother...

They learn how to blend in…

How to make the most of their leisure time...

How to keep their head above water...

And how to keep their nose clean...

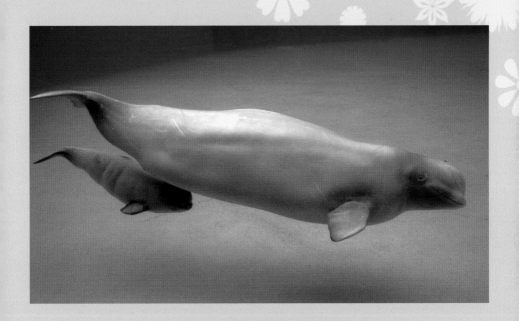

Sometimes children must watch and learn from Mother…

Whether it's basic table manners...

Or refining the perfect posture...

Children learn so much by following Mother's lead...

And they soon learn to work as a team...

MOTHER'S PRIDE

It's natural for a mother to show her children off...

Every child is her pride and joy...

And each one is beautiful in its mother's eyes...

She'll admire them from every conceivable angle...

To ensure they're flawless from top to toe...

Mothers can't stand their kids looking grubby…

The cleaning process waits for no-one...

Even when the kids kick up a fuss...

It can be a laborious task...

Unless you've got the right equipment...

Kids can be demanding at times…

And they don't always consider your comfort...

Or know when to leave you alone…

But though they do get in the way from time to time...

A mother's tolerance knows no bounds...

Sometimes, of course, enough is enough…

And a mother's temper can be as fierce as her love...

A child needs a strong word every so often…

But a mother's scolding is part of growing up...

And they always make up in the end...

It can be a treacherous world out there...

And mothers know the safety of home ground...

It's a mother's instinct to keep a watchful eye...

And stop the kids running wild…

Even if they start to sulk…

Mothers shoulder their burdens with patience...

And a firm hand...

To some kids it comes easily…

Others take time to grasp it...

And to some, it just never comes naturally...

Mothers love to be seen out with their kids…

And will happily let them tag along…

Whether it's on the school run…

The weekly shop…

Or just a walk in the woods...

Children love it when Mother finds time to play…

Whether it's hide and seek…

Or a blinking contest...

You can have a lot of fun with Mother...

But she decides when playtime's over…

Mothers keep their children safe and sound...

They're always on the lookout for potential dangers…

They like to keep them where they can see them…

Mother's protection inspires confidence…

Though occasionally there's a little too much bravado…

Our mother is the one we run to for comfort...

She knows all the right things to say…

She soothes our pain…

Eases our discomfort…

And reassures us…

Children can be such chatterboxes...

And they all want to tell their side of the story…

Though they can be prone to exaggeration…

Or just a little shy to speak out...

They know that mothers make the best listeners...

Mothers love to spend quality time with their children...

It's a chance to enjoy each other's company…

Whether it's at home...

Or out at the park...

They always share that special bond…

Mothers love to be photographed with their kids...

They can have a real hoot in front of the camera...

They always want to show their best side...

And to avoid rocking the boat…

When in doubt, just say cheese…

A mother's love soothes and lulls…

Children know they'll be safe in their mother's arms...

Or, in fact, anywhere near her...

Bedtime is a chance for Mother to relax too...

In fact, being a mother can be an exhausting job…